This book is to be returned on or before
the last date

D03335258

People who have helped the world

MARTIN LUTHER KING

by Valerie Schloredt & Pam Brown

OTHER TITLES IN THE SERIES

Robert Baden-Powell by Julia Courtney (1-85015-180-6)
Louis Braille by Beverley Birch (1-85015-139-3)
Marie Curie by Beverley Birch (1-85015-092-3)
The Dalai Lama by Christopher Gibb (1-85015-141-5)
Father Damien by Pam Brown (1-85015-084-2)
Henry Dunant by Pam Brown (1-85015-106-7)
Mahatma Gandhi by Michael Nicholson (1-85015-091-5)
Bob Geldof by Charlotte Gray (1-85015-085-0)
Mikhail Gorbachev by Anna Sproule (1-85015-218-7)
Maria Montessori by Michael Pollard (1-85015-211-X)
Florence Nightingale by Pam Brown (1-85015-117-2)
Louis Pasteur by Beverley Birch (1-85015-140-7)
Albert Schweitzer by James Bentley (1-85015-114-8)
Sir Peter Scott by Julia Courtney (1-85015-108-3)
Mother Teresa by Charlotte Gray (1-85015-093-1)
Desmond Tutu by David Winner (1-85015-087-7)
Lech Walesa by Mary Craig (1-85015-107-5)
Raoul Wallenberg by Michael Nicholson and
    David Winner (1-85015-109-1)
Peter Benenson by David Winner (1-185015-217-9)
Charles Chaplin by Pam Brown (1-85015-143-1)
Abraham Lincoln by Anna Sproule (1-85015-155-5)
Nelson Mandela by Benjamin Pogrund (1-85015-239-X)
Eleanor Roosevelt by David Winner (1-85015-142-3)
Helen Keller by Fiona Macdonald (1-85015-252-7)

Picture Credits
All pictures, including the cover, except those listed below, are © Flip Schulke or from the Schulke Archives, Florida. The Publishers gratefully acknowledge his permission to reproduce them.
BBC Hulton Picture Library: 4 (both); Black Star, New York: Charles Moore 30 (below), 45 (both); Rex Features: 8, 9; Val Wilmer: 6. Map drawn by Geoff Pleasance.
The Publishers have been unable to identify the owner of the picture of Gandhi on page 12; any information which would allow them to do so, would be much appreciated.

The Publishers thank Joan Daves for permission to reprint material Copyright © 1955, 1956, 1963 by Martin Luther King, Jr.; Copyright © 1968 by Estate of Martin Luther King, Jr. The Publishers also wish to express their gratitude to Flip Schulke, King's friend and photographer, for advice in preparing the text and for clarifying points in the story. Without his assistance, the task of preparing this book would have been much more difficult.

Published in Great Britain in 1988 by
Exley Publications Ltd,
16 Chalk Hill, Watford,
Herts WD1 4BN, United Kingdom.

Second printing 1989
Third and fourth printings 1990
Fifth printing 1994
Copyright © Exley Publications, 1988

British Library Cataloguing in Publication Data
Schloredt, Valerie with Pam Brown.
  Martin Luther King –
  (People who have helped the world).
  1. King, Martin Luther. – Juvenile
    literature.
  2. Afro-Americans – Biography –
    Juvenile literature.
  3. Baptists – Clergy – Biography –
    Juvenile literature.
  4. Clergy – United States – Biography –
    Juvenile literature.
  I. Title.
  II. Series.
  323.1'196'024   E.185.97.K5

Series conceived and edited by Helen Exley
Picture research: Diana Briscoe.
Research: Margaret Montgomery.
Editing: Pam Brown.
Typeset by Brush Off Studios,
St Albans, Herts AL3 4PH.
Printed and bound in Hungary.

ISBN 1-85015-086-9

MARTIN LUTHER KING

America's great non-violent leader, who was murdered in the struggle for black rights

**Valerie Schloredt
& Pam Brown**

Above: The horror and the reality of slavery. Dragged from their villages and their families by armed raiders and chained together in irons, African slaves were shipped off to a life of toil and exploitation. Slavery in the United States ended with President Abraham Lincoln's proclamation in 1863. Slavery still flourished in other parts of the world and this photograph of captured slaves was taken in West Africa in the 1890s.

Right: Fifteen million people were shipped across the Atlantic and chained to lie horizontally on their wood bunks throughout the voyage. Huge numbers died. Martin Luther King, Jr.'s grandfather was a slave.

4

Slavery

For thousands of European immigrants in the 1800s, North America meant freedom, hope, the chance of a new life. For many black people, it meant an auctioneer selling them off like so many cattle.

"Here's a fine healthy girl. Lots of flesh on her. Good teeth. Open your mouth, nigger – muscle enough to do a good day's work in the field and intelligent enough to be trained to the house. Fine breeding stock. What am I bid?"

African people had been torn away from their homes and families in far-off lands, to be jammed together, chained and terrified, in the stench and darkness of the holds of sailing ships. Those ships brought them to America where they were sold as slaves. Sold to a lifetime as someone's property, their children sold in time to distant strangers if the master so wished, husbands sold away from wives, wives from husbands. At best treated as a well-loved dog, at worst worked without mercy; beaten, humiliated, mutilated, or killed outright.

Emancipation

Eventually many people in the United States came to believe that slavery was wrong, that all human beings had a right to be free. They believed that no human should be allowed to own another. But they could not convince everyone that slavery should be made illegal. Finally in the 1860s a war was fought to free the slaves. It was called the Civil War or the War Between the States. In 1863, before the end of that war, slavery was abolished and black people were emancipated – or set free.

After the war, the US became rich and powerful, a place of opportunity and success. But at the edges of the great cities were the run-down shanty-towns

"... we have in common with all other men a natural right to our freedoms without being deprived of them by our fellow men as we are a freeborn people and have never forfeited this blessing by any compact or agreement whatever. But we were unjustly dragged by the cruel hand of power from our dearest friends and some of us stolen from the bosoms of our tender parents and from a populous pleasant and plentiful country and brought hither to be made slaves for life in a Christian land. Thus we are deprived of everything that hath a tendency to make life even tolerable ..."

from "A Slave Petition for Freedom," 1774.

5

After the Civil War, black people were supposed to be free, but they had no land. All the land was owned by whites; in reality, the black people remained trapped by poverty. When the United States was hit by depression in the 1930s, the black people suffered most of all.

where the black people lived – slaves no longer, but often second-class citizens, despised, ignored and doing the jobs no one else wanted.

In the southern states especially, where the great cotton plantations had devoured generation upon generation of black people, they could, in 1963, be worse off than they had been in 1863 when slavery had been abolished. Ignorant whites prided themselves that they were a superior race – and that every black, however intelligent and decent, was an inferior human being. They addressed every black man, however old and dignified, as "Boy." Even the more sensible whites were so trapped in generations of prejudice that often they too regarded black people as different: as backward children, given to laziness and lies, to be treated with kindly condescension if they behaved themselves and "knew their place."

"Jim Crow"

The black people who had got away to the North and found education and good jobs were still, in

6

the eyes of too many men and women, "niggers." When Paul Robeson, one of the finest singers in the world, went to give concerts in the South, he was refused entrance to some hotels. While whites would buy expensive tickets to hear him sing, many were horrified at the thought of sitting in the same restaurant with him.

After the Civil War, the southern states passed laws that separated blacks and whites, and helped to keep blacks poor and unequal. These laws were called "Jim Crow" after the name of a well-known minstrel song.

No black person could eat in a white person's restaurant or café, or sit on a seat reserved for whites. In some places it was a crime for blacks and whites to play cards together. The religious whites approved of the blacks going to church, but well away from their own, as if God too did not regard them as being of equal value.

"Among white women who worked, one of ten was employed as a maid; among black women, six of ten were so employed.... The Negro mortality rate was nearly twice that for whites. In Washington D.C., for which statistics were typical, the infant mortality rate among whites was thirty-seven, among blacks seventy-one."

Richard Pollenberg, from "One Nation Divisible."

KKK

Worse, after the Civil War, a terrible organization had been founded, called the Ku Klux Klan (KKK). That sounds like a childish name, but it was, and is, a vicious organization.

Like Nazis, the members of the KKK believe themselves to be a superior race and delight in ritual and show. They hold their ceremonies in front of a blazing cross and wear white robes with very pointed hoods that would be ridiculous if they did not hide such evil. The KKK could lynch a black man for the mere suspicion of having laid hands on a white woman, yet white men thought it almost a game to attack black women and were never punished. Even today the KKK are blatant in their violence, believing that their friends in high places will protect them.

For years, brave men and women had struggled for justice and equality for black people. There had been great courage and great suffering. Here and there, there had been victories, but still there was so much to be done. Black people needed a movement and a leader to win them the freedom that

"Jim Crow meant more than physical separation. Separate waiting rooms at bus stations, separate railroad cars, separate sections in movie theaters, separate schools and churches, separate restaurants and drinking fountains – these were the system's most visible manifestations, but there were more subtle ones as well. Social conventions that implied mutual respect, such as shaking hands or tipping one's hat, were taboo."

Richard Pollenberg, from "One Nation Divisible."

Members of the infamous Ku Klux Klan operated quite openly in many of the southern states. Many of them held positions in the police forces and so were able to hold up any serious investigations into crimes committed by the Klan. This photograph was taken in the 1980s and although the KKK has lost power, it is still active in some southern states.

President Abraham Lincoln had promised during the Civil War.

Some black leaders had become so exasperated by the long delays that they advocated violence and revenge – armed risings against injustice. But one great leader, Dr. Martin Luther King, knew that this would make everyone believe that black people were no better than those who were causing their misery; it would be to act as if black people did not deserve the respect and equality they asked for. In the 1950s and 1960s, Dr. King led his people in massive non-violent demonstrations that changed the attitudes of millions of people in the US and throughout the world.

Opposite: This is a modern photograph of the Ku Klux Klan. KKK ceremonies still have strange rituals, such as the burning of a fiery cross, to create fear in their communities. The fear the Ku Klux Klan evoked used to stem not so much from their strange costumes as from their willingness to use the ultimate weapon of murder. During the first thirty years of this century, hundreds of black men and women were lynched by white gangs – hanged in public and frequently burned alive. The number of lynchings had fallen away by the 1950s and 1960s, but they still happened. The fear was still there.

A childhood in the church

Martin Luther King, Jr., was born on the fifteenth of January, 1929, in Atlanta, Georgia, a city in the deep South of the US. He was named after his father, and the family, which was made up of his parents, a doting grandmother and a brother and sister, called him ML for short – a nickname that stuck throughout his childhood.

Because he was a minister, a preacher, ML's father, "Daddy King," had an important position in the black community. The Church played a vital role in the life of blacks in the American South. It was the heart of the black community, the source of inspiration and comfort for people whose lives were hard the other six days of the week.

Black preachers had a fine sense of the dramatic. The congregation quivered at the descriptions of the horrors that awaited the wicked in hell and rejoiced at the glories promised to the good. They responded with great enthusiasm, punctuating the preacher's words with cries of "Hallelujah!" "Amen!" and "Praise the Lord!" – swept away by the faith and enthusiasm. Everyone, from the small children to the very old, joined in singing the beautiful gospel songs that had been made up by their ancestors in the days of slavery, when comfort and courage had been hard to find.

Young ML was a clever boy. At five, he was memorizing passages from the Bible. At six, he would sing the Gospel songs for the congregation. And all the time he was learning.

One day, after hearing a guest minister give an impressive sermon, ML told his parents "Some day, I'm going to get me some big words like that!"

Growing up with racism

Like all black children, his childhood and youth were scarred by racial prejudice. Every day, little things made it clear to him that to be black was to be a second-class citizen. For instance, when he was only a little boy, he was suddenly told not to play with two white friends. Their mother sent him home, saying that her children were getting too old to play with a black child. Martin's parents explained that he should *never* believe he was inferior, because he *wasn't*. It was simply ignorance and prejudice that made otherwise decent people behave in this way. But Martin was deeply hurt. And the boys who had been happy to be his friends were set on the road to believing that all black people were different and inferior.

As he grew up, Martin learned that segregation – the two races living completely separated lives – was a fact of life in the South. As a black person he could only use certain public drinking fountains and toilets; the others had signs hanging in front of them saying "Whites Only." If he wanted an ice cream cone, he was sent to a side window outside

Martin Luther King was born in Atlanta, Georgia, in this comfortable house on Auburn Avenue. His grandmother had worked as a cleaning "girl" for a wealthy white banker, and "Daddy King," Martin's father, was determined that his family would have a better life. Walking past the white banker's house one day, "Daddy King" vowed that he, too, would have a big house, even a bigger one. He, too, would be a director of a bank. He succeeded.

the shop. When he wanted to see a film, he couldn't sit downstairs – that was reserved for whites – but had to go up to the back balcony. Blacks and whites did not go to school together, or use the same public library or the same parks. Blacks never lived in white areas. Maya Angelou, a famous black writer, says that when she was a little girl in the South, she just didn't realize white people were human beings like black people; they seemed so remote and strange.

A bitter moment

The most humiliating incident occurred when Martin was 15 and in his final year of high school. He belonged to the school's debating society and had gone with the society to a contest in another town, where he won a prize for his speech "The Negro and the Constitution." It was a proud moment, and he was happy and pleased as he and his teacher rode home on the bus that night.

As the bus went on, more passengers boarded until all the seats were taken. Then two white passengers got on, and the bus driver demanded that Martin and his teacher stand and give up their seats. Martin refused, but the driver insisted, calling him a "black bastard." This made Martin terribly angry. He had just been awarded a prize for his speech on black people's rights, yet here were the very same constitutional rights he had spoken about being pushed aside and forgotten.

He felt like fighting, but he was with his teacher, who was frightened and begging him to stand up and avoid trouble. There was very little Martin could do at that moment, so he stood up, furious at having to give in. It was one of the bitterest moments he had ever known.

Lessons from Daddy King

Besides being a minister, Reverend King was a shrewd businessman, and the family lived well. But being a minister and reasonably well-to-do meant nothing to the local white community; to them this

In everyday life, most of the Ku Klux Klan members looked like ordinary, respectable citizens. They were often churchgoers and community leaders. This photograph, taken in the 1950s, shows how the children were still being brought up with the same prejudices against black people.

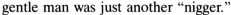

gentle man was just another "nigger."

But Martin's father knew how to respond to insults. When a policeman stopped him on the road one day and said "Boy, let me see your license," the Reverend King pointed to his son and said "See that child there? That is a *boy*, I am a man." He ran a great risk of being called "uppity," but his son admired his courage and his dignity.

He would always remember what his father said about racism: "I don't care how long I have to live with the system. I am never going to accept it. I'll fight it till I die."

"On the one hand, my mother taught me that I should feel a sense of somebodiness. On the other hand, I had to go out and face the system, which stared me in the face everyday, saying 'You are less than.' 'You are not equal to.' So there was a real tension within."

Martin Luther King, Jr., from "King Remembered."

College days

Martin had begun college when he was fifteen, three years earlier than most. He went to Morehouse College in Atlanta, one of the best black colleges in the country, where open discussion of racial matters was encouraged. He knew just how lucky he was compared to so many black youngsters, and he made the most of his chances.

His father had set his heart on Martin's following him into the Church, but Martin himself thought he might like to become a doctor or a lawyer, professions he felt would be of more use to his people. But the President of the college, Dr. Benjamin Mays, was a minister who thought the Church should play a greater role in US society. The combination of learning and inspiration in his sermons impressed Martin and made him change his mind. A minister like Dr. Mays could help people in all sorts of ways, dealing with real modern problems.

So Martin told his father that, after all, he would become a minister. His father organized a trial sermon for Martin at his own church, the Ebenezer Baptist Church in Atlanta, and large crowds arrived that Sunday to hear the seventeen-year-old preach. He was very nervous because he did not want to let his father down in front of their own people, but he did well. Later that same year he was ordained and made assistant minister to his father. But his education was far from over. He wanted to continue his studies at a college in the North.

Martin Luther King believed very strongly that American blacks should adopt the methods of non-violence advocated by Mahatma Gandhi, the father of Indian independence. Non-violent protest did not mean being passive. It meant total, organized, non-cooperation with evil, a willingness to suffer for what is right, a willingness to pack the jails and, if necessary, a willingness to die for the cause.

Philosophy of non-violence

It was in 1948 that Martin enrolled at the Crozer Seminary in Pennsylvania. He worked hard and in his spare time read the work of famous theologians – people who write about religion – and philosophers – people who write about the meaning of life. The philosopher who impressed him most was Henry Thoreau who was an abolitionist, a man who believed that slavery *must* be ended. He served a jail sentence because he refused to pay taxes to a government that allowed slavery to continue, and in 1849 he wrote a famous essay, "On the Duty of Civil Disobedience," explaining why he had made this stand against what he believed to be a shocking, unacceptable, social injustice.

But the man whose beliefs most excited Martin Luther King was Mahatma Gandhi. His philosophy of non-violence, or soul-force, pitted the spiritual strength of India's people against the political and military strength of imperialist Britain. The Indians

Ebenezer Baptist Church in Atlanta, Georgia, was Martin's father's church. Martin grew up with the strong influence of this successful and well-attended church. He did not like the emotional style of the preachers nor the hand-clapping and shouted responses of the congregation. It was here at Ebenezer Baptist Church that Martin preached his own first sermon. His style was calmer, more serious, than that of the other ministers, but he was immediately recognized as a great preacher.

In 1948, at nineteen, King obtained a degree in sociology and went on to study for a degree in divinity at Crozer Seminary, in Pennsylvania. As one of only six blacks among almost a hundred students living in a cloistered, somewhat solemn community, he was ill at ease. "I'm afraid I was grimly serious for a time. I had a tendency to overdress, to keep my room spotless, my shoes perfectly shined and my clothes immaculately pressed." He was very successful, earning A's in every course.

demonstrated over and over again that they did not want to be governed by a foreign power, benevolent or not. They wanted to make their own decisions, correct or not.

Gandhi said that although they must be willing to die for independence, they must not kill for it – however harshly they were treated.

Now Martin began to believe that what had succeeded in India might also succeed in the US. But as yet it was just an idea at the back of his head. He had no thought that one day he would lead a vast civil rights movement – a campaign for justice for black people in the US – with non-violence as its great guiding principle.

Martin meets Coretta

Martin graduated at the top of his class from Crozer and went on to continue his studies at Boston University. He began working for his doctorate, or Ph.D. degree, and enrolled in an advanced course in the philosophy of religion, studying Hinduism, Shintoism and Islam, as well as Christianity.

As serious as he was about his studies, Martin still found time to enjoy himself. He was a charming young man – and like most charming young men, had plenty of girlfriends. But the fun of going out with so many different girls began to wear thin; he wished he could find someone special, someone who could share his life and his hopes.

Then a friend introduced him to a young singer named Coretta Scott. She came from the South, like Martin, having grown up in a black farming family in Alabama. A scholarship had allowed her to study music at the New England Conservatory, and she was working part-time to pay her living expenses. The very last thing she wanted was to be swept off her feet and give up her career. Marriage and children were things she hoped to have – but *after* she had established herself in music.

The right woman

But all her sensible plans went out of the window. At first, Martin seemed to her to be too short – he was five foot seven – but the more time she spent with him the more she liked him.

Martin himself was bowled over by her beauty and intelligence, her vivid personality, her strength of character. He told her so!

The more they saw of each other, the more they felt for each other, and, on June 18, 1953, they were married by Martin's father at Coretta's home in Marion.

Back in Boston later that year, Martin and Coretta finished their last year of studies, and Martin began looking for a job. He was happy in the academic life and wanted to teach theology at a college or university, but thought he should work as a minister for a few years first.

Back South

The best offer Martin received was from the Dexter Avenue Baptist Church in Montgomery, Alabama, where the congregation was looking for a new minister. Dexter Avenue was a solid brick building that had been built just after the Civil War. The membership was small, only about 400, but well-educated. Some of the congregation were teachers at the black college in Montgomery.

Martin's first position as a minister was at Dexter Avenue Baptist Church in Montgomery, Alabama, a church built just after the end of the Civil War. He was only twenty-five at the time and, understandably, he was reluctant to return to the South again to face all the bitterness of segregation.

In deciding whether to take the position at Dexter Avenue, Martin faced the prospect of moving south again, back to segregation, discrimination, and the threat of violence that hung over blacks in the South. Coretta had grown up in Alabama, and she knew how bad conditions for black people were there. On the other hand, the South was still home for both of them, and they had family there. Martin felt that, after the advantages of education they had received, it was their duty to go back to try to improve things if they could. They talked it over and decided to move back to the South – at least for a few years.

In September of 1954, Martin and Coretta settled into the parsonage that served the black community of Montgomery. They had a busy life together.

Martin woke at 5:30 each morning to work on his doctoral thesis for three hours before breakfast. He then drove downtown to the Dexter Avenue Church, where his duties as minister included giving advice to members of his congregation on family problems, performing marriage ceremonies and funeral services, and serving as a character witness in matters of business and law.

As a boy he had sometimes been embarrassed by his father's emotional style of preaching, but now Martin began to see that he could combine both learning and emotion in his sermons. He began to use dramatic phrases and timing to make his point, sometimes speaking softly and quietly, and sometimes with a thunderous voice that vibrated through the church. People came to church to be uplifted and inspired, and this is what Martin tried to do every Sunday. He was a very good preacher, and already showed signs of becoming a great orator. He soon became immensely popular with his congregation.

Happy times

In the spring of 1955, Martin finished his thesis and went north to Boston to receive his degree. He was awarded a doctorate in theology and was from then

Most of the important events in this book took place in the southern states. Many of these states had permitted slavery before the Civil War and fought on the Confederate side in that war. Black people make up 11% of the population of the United States. Most of them used to live in the southern states, but now 47%, nearly half, live in the northern states.

THE EASTERN UNITED STATES OF AMERICA

on known as either "Dr." or "Reverend" King.

There was another cause of celebration that spring: Coretta was expecting their first child, Yolanda, the first of their four children. It was a happy time for the young family, and they were making new friends in the town.

Life in the quiet, sleepy town went on happily for Dr. King and his family, but he was only too well aware of what lay below the surface of that peaceful-seeming community.

The need for change

The position of black people in Montgomery was typical of many other areas of the South. The segregation system meant that black and white children had to attend different schools, and the black

17

schools were far poorer than the white.

The Supreme Court of the United States had decided in 1954 that this could not be allowed to continue. The law said all Americans should have the same opportunities. The Court judges said segregation in schools must stop, that black and white children should be educated together on equal terms. They even added the words "with all deliberate speed" to try to hurry the process. But it was easier said than done. The southern whites were horrified at the idea, and nothing whatever had been done to put the ruling into effect in Montgomery.

Schooling was not the only problem. In theory the blacks could vote exactly as the whites, but all sorts of rules had been brought in locally to make it difficult for them. The poor and uneducated blacks were asked to pay poll taxes and to pass literacy tests. If regulations did not stop them from voting, then the white people turned to threats and violence. Most black people in the South could only get menial jobs as manual workers or servants. If it was discovered that black people had tried to vote or to stand up for their rights, they could find themselves out of a job. So while there were about forty thousand black people in Montgomery who were entitled to vote, only about two thousand were registered.

Years of threats, cruelty and insult had made many of the black population afraid to stand up for themselves in even the smallest way. The only way to stay alive and to make some sort of life for themselves and their families was to keep quiet and accept what came, hoping perhaps for better things in Heaven. The young Martin Luther King saw his people cowed, submissive, afraid, and he knew better things could never come in this world if they went on accepting such a life.

Back of the bus

You remember how Martin had to stand up for a white man on a bus when he was a boy? How hurt and indignant he had been?

Things had not improved. In a way the methods by which the bus companies in Montgomery were run summed up all the evils of segregation.

The city would not have black bus drivers, and segregation on the buses themselves was strict, even more than in other southern states. Blacks were allowed to sit at the back only, though they were permitted to move in to the middle section if the seats were empty and no whites wanted them. The first four rows were absolutely forbidden to blacks at all times and were under a "Whites Only" sign. If the bus began to fill up, any blacks in the middle section had to stand up so that white passengers could sit down. Young white men could expect and insist that an old lady burdened with shopping, or a pregnant girl, or a disabled person, give up their seat for them.

To make them feel even more inferior, black people had to pay their fare at the front of the bus, then get off and board the bus again at the back. This was to prevent them from offending white passengers by walking through *their* section.

It is no wonder that these rules were a source of resentment in the black population. A little over a year after the Reverend King had come to Montgomery, he was to lead the battle that put an end to such humiliation.

The Rosa Parks incident

On the evening of December 1, 1955, a black lady named Rosa Parks left the downtown department store where she worked as a seamstress and walked to the bus stop to catch the bus that would take her home. The first one that came was already full, and some black passengers were standing at the back, so she decided to let that bus go. She boarded the next one, and although all the seats in the back section were already taken, she found an empty seat in the middle section and sat down.

The rule was that if even one white person sat down in that section, all the blacks seated there were expected to get up. At the third bus stop, a handful of white passengers got on and took all the

Mrs. Rosa Parks, sitting in a bus, after the boycott in Montgomery, Alabama. Most people who used the buses were black, and the white drivers often insulted them, especially the women, calling them "niggers," "apes," and "black cows." Blacks were not allowed in the first four rows of the bus and they had to stand if whites needed seats. One day, it was all too much for Mrs. Parks. She was no great agitator, but she was tired and her feet hurt. She refused to get up. She was arrested, and a huge boycott of the buses had begun.

remaining "Whites Only" seats at the front of the bus. One white man remained standing, and the bus driver turned around to where Mrs. Parks and three other black passengers were sitting. "I need those seats," he said. None of the black passengers moved until he turned around a second time and added threateningly, "You all better make it light on yourselves and let me have those seats." The other three got up, but Mrs. Parks stayed seated. The bus driver turned around again.

"You going to stand up?" he said. "I'll have you arrested if you don't." Mrs. Parks was tired. She had had a long, hard day, and there seemed no good reason at all why one man should need more than one seat. Something snapped in Mrs. Parks at that moment. Perhaps the patience with which she had endured years of subservience and insult. She settled herself firmly in the seat and said "Go ahead then – *have* me arrested."

As the other passengers looked on with curiosity, alarm, disapproval, or even admiration, Mrs. Parks waited while the bus driver got out to find a policeman. The policeman arrived and asked Mrs. Parks why she hadn't stood up. "I didn't think I should have to," she replied, adding, "Why do you push us around?"

"I don't know" replied the policeman, "but the law is the law and you are under arrest."

Mrs. Parks under arrest

Mrs. Parks didn't look like a person to challenge the law of Montgomery. She was a quiet-looking lady, wearing small steel-rimmed spectacles, but like thousands of other black people who rode the buses day after day, she was weary of being treated with such contempt.

Much later she was asked if she had planned her protest. "No" she answered, "I was just plain tired, and my feet hurt."

Mrs. Parks' patience had given way, had she but known it, at the best possible moment.

Everyone knew that Mrs. Parks was a good, quiet, hard–working, upstanding member of the

Opposite: During his time in Montgomery, Martin Luther King learned to appreciate just how important the Church could be in giving black people a sense of dignity. Here they were free of the white man, free of unjust laws, free to gain spiritual strength on their own ground. "Any religion that professes to be concerned with the souls of men and is not concerned with the slums that damn them and the social conditions that cripple them is a dry-as-dust religion," Martin Luther King declared. His reputation as a preacher soon spread far beyond Montgomery.

black community; people were bound to support her cause. Here at last was an issue to unite the black people of Montgomery and all the white people who believed the system to be wrong. Martin Luther King agreed with enthusiasm to lend his full support.

The leaders had been wondering whether to boycott the bus services. This would mean that no black person would travel on any bus. Not only would it bring the end of segregation to the notice of everyone in America, but it would deprive the bus company of a great deal of money.

Mrs. Parks' defiance had made this the perfect time to take action.

The boycott plan

They had to work quickly, while indignation was strong. The black ministers and leaders met together on the Friday after Rosa Parks' arrest and decided that Monday was the time to begin the boycott. The ministers were to spread the news at the Sunday services, and a committee was to prepare a leaflet to be circulated in every black area. Clearly and firmly, it gave the news of Mrs. Parks' arrest and said,

"Don't ride the buses to work, to town, to school, or anywhere on Monday.... If you work, take a cab or share a ride, or walk. Come to a mass meeting, Monday at 7:00 p.m., at the Holt Street Baptist Church for further instruction."

Another committee got to work contacting all the black-owned taxi companies in Montgomery, asking them to help the boycott by carrying passengers for the usual bus fare of just ten cents. The taxi firms, with a total of 210 cars between them, agreed to the plan. The stage was set for Monday's bus boycott.

The first day

Martin Luther King got up early on the morning of December 5, 1955, the first day of the boycott. He was still in the kitchen drinking his morning

coffee when the first bus, which was normally crammed with black passengers on their way to work, rolled past the house. Coretta called him to their front window. The bus was empty. The black people of Montgomery were staying off the buses, and the boycott was under way.

King drove through the streets of Montgomery that morning to check on the progress of the boycott. Things were going even better than he had dared hope. Blacks throughout the city were walking miles to work rather than take a bus. Many were hitchhiking, or sharing rides. Some were even riding mules or horse-drawn carriages into town!

About 17,500 black passengers normally used Montgomery's buses, making up 75% of the bus company's customers. Today, groups of people gathered at the bus stops to watch the buses pull up – and leave empty of passengers. There were jeers and laughter, but although the police were out keeping a close watch on the bus stops, there

The blacks in Montgomery refused to ride the buses by the thousand, and car pools were formed among all those who had cars to help people get to work. Some people preferred to walk, as a demonstration against injustice. One old woman, hobbling along with great difficulty, was offered a ride one day, but declined it, saying, "I'm not walking for myself. I'm walking for my children and my grandchildren."

*Opposite: Martin Luther
King at home with Coretta
and their children. He was
often away and he worried
that his civil rights work was
robbing his children of the
time a father should have
with them. So when he was
home, he tried to set aside
prime time to be with them
all. Above the family is a
photograph of Mahatma
Gandhi, King's greatest
hero.*

was no sign of violence or intimidation. The bus
boycott was a peaceful act of protest and one that
gave the black community a new feeling of strength
and unity – and hope for better things to come.

That afternoon, the leaders met to decide the
next move. They formed a new organization, the
Montgomery Improvement Association, to keep an
eye on the boycott and, to Dr. King's surprise,
elected him president. He was only 26, but they
recognized that he was the best man for the job.
His first task was to address the mass meeting to
be held that evening.

King's speech

When King arrived at the church, he found a huge
crowd milling around outside the building. People
had been arriving since 5:00 p.m., and all the seats
inside were already taken. Loudspeakers had been
rigged up outside the church to broadcast the meeting to the people standing outside. Police drove
slowly around the church, keeping watch over the
crowd, expecting, perhaps hoping for, trouble.

The meeting began with a rousing chorus of "On-
ward Christian Soldiers." Then Rosa Parks came
forward to tell the story of her refusal to give up
her seat and the arrest that followed. The crowd
applauded and cheered her, and then it was Dr.
King's turn. He looked out over a sea of expectant
faces. There were about 4,000 people attending the
meeting, as well as photographers, reporters and
television crews.

He began his speech by describing the way blacks
had been treated on Montgomery's buses. They had
suffered the brutalities of segregation for a long
time, but, he said: "There comes a time when
people get tired. We are here this evening to say
to those who have mistreated us for so long that
we are tired – tired of being segregated and
humiliated – tired of being kicked about by the
brutal feet of oppression."

The audience listened intently as he went on to
stress the need for unity in their action, saying, "If
we are united, we can get many of the things that

King was a passionate, persuasive orator who was regarded by many to be the greatest in the United States. His sermons and speeches were his most powerful weapon as a leader and they led thousands of people to take action for black civil rights. He believed that laws could and should be broken openly, in full view of everyone, with the protester bravely taking the consequences. "There comes a time when a moral man can't obey a law which his conscience tells him is unjust. And the important thing is that when he does that, he willingly accepts the consequences."

we not only desire, but which we justly deserve." He stressed the justice of their cause, saying, "If we are wrong, the Supreme Court of this nation is wrong. If we are wrong, the Constitution of the United States is wrong. If we are wrong, God Almighty is wrong. If we are wrong, Jesus of Nazareth was merely a utopian dreamer who never came down to Earth. If we are wrong, justice is a lie."

The crowd was completely at one with King now, hanging on every word. He cautioned them about the dangers they faced. There could be no violence on their part in this struggle; he said, "We will be guided by the highest principles of law and order." The Christian ideal of love should also guide their actions: "In spite of the mistreatment that we have confronted, we must not become bitter and end up hating our white brothers."

He finished speaking and sat down. The crowd burst into an uproar of singing and cheering. They had found a cause, they had found unity, they had

found hope, they had found their leader. He had drawn them together at last, and they understood their power to obtain justice and dignity. It was the first time that people had seen what a great leader Martin Luther King was to become.

Three demands

Ralph Abernathy, King's close friend and associate in the civil rights campaign, rose next to read out the list of three demands the Montgomery Improvement Association wanted to present to city officials and the bus company. The boycott would continue until these demands were met:

1) Bus drivers would treat black passengers with courtesy.
2) Passengers would be seated on a first-come, first-serve basis, with blacks beginning from the back and whites from the front.

"His greatest personal contribution was interpreting the situation to the mass of the people. He could speak better than any man that I've ever heard in expressing to the people their problem and making them see clearly what the situation was and inspiring them to work at it."

Rufus Lewis,
a Montgomery businessman.

27

3) The bus company must immediately hire black drivers on routes through black areas.

King asked the crowd to approve these conditions: "All in favor, let it be known by standing on your feet."

There was a great surge as every person in the huge crowd stood up. The civil rights movement in the US had begun.

Throughout the civil rights movement there were many whites standing side-by-side with blacks in their fight for justice. When King mobilized the black community, he constantly demanded from his followers an absence of bitterness. When the bus boycott was over, he said to the crowd, "I would be terribly disappointed if any of you go back to the buses bragging, 'We, the Negroes, won a victory over the white people.' We must take this not as victory over the white man but as a victory for justice and democracy."

The first rainy day

The bus boycott was well under way, and Reverend King and other black leaders arranged to meet city officials to discuss the dispute. But right away it became clear that neither the city nor the bus company had any intention of desegregating the buses. The Mayor said smugly, "Comes the first rainy day and the Negroes will be back on the buses."

How wrong he was. The black people had found the road to freedom, and no downpour was going to break their spirit. But they realized this was to be no quick victory; there was a long fight ahead.

The police soon put an end to the 10-cent taxi

service, but the Montgomery Improvement Association had arranged a city-wide motor pool. Car owners took people to and from work, and black churches served as pick-up points. The system ran like clockwork, although many people still walked to work.

The protest was visible – what people call "high profile." All those black people trudging to and from work, whatever the weather, became a clear symbol of their new-found dignity. No one could ignore this protest against injustice.

One frail, elderly lady, "Old Mother Pollard," walked with as much determination as the rest. One day after service, Dr. King asked her if she wasn't getting tired of walking. "My feet is tired," she replied, "but my soul is rested."

The new spirit awakened by the boycott made every effort seem worthwhile. As they had hoped, the attention of the world was caught by this quiet, dogged, peaceful protest. The focus of press, radio and television coverage was not only Montgomery's buses, but the whole question of racial oppression in the United States. And Martin Luther King was seen as a most powerful leader of the black cause.

The get-tough policy

The publicity made the militant white segregationists even angrier. The world was laughing at them. They were made to look like fools by a bunch of "uppity niggers."

The three most powerful men in Montgomery – the Mayor, the Police Chief and the City Commissioner – announced that they had joined the deeply racist "White Citizens' Council." The mayor said that from now on the city would adopt what he called a "get-tough policy."

Now the white bullies began to show their true natures. Car-pool drivers were stopped by the police for any reason, or none at all. People waiting to be picked up were threatened with arrest for hitchhiking.

Martin Luther King, himself, was arrested on a charge of driving at 30 mph in a 25 mph zone. He

"If we don't stop helping these African flesh eaters, we will soon wake up and find Reverend King in the White House."

from a leaflet circulated by white racists.

Ku Klux Klan member. The KKK and the White Citizens Council continued to threaten and intimidate the campaigners. One anonymous note that came to King said "If you allow the niggers to go back on the buses and sit in the front seats, we're going to burn down fifty houses in one night, including yours."

Above: White racist groups were particularly active in Birmingham, Alabama, which was called "the most racist city in America."

Below: Ku Klux Klan signboard greeting visitors to a small town in Alabama.

spent a few hours in jail before being released on bail – the first of many arrests. He was to spend many hours in prison during his years as a civil rights leader.

The police could use the law only to intimidate, but some white extremists did not mean to have their hands tied by any law.

By January, King and his family were being bombarded with hate mail, thirty or forty threatening letters a day. They burned them, but it was terrible to be faced by such blind, unprovoked hatred. These were the first murder threats received by Coretta and Martin. It was only the beginning of years of living with fear.

Telephone calls, too. All day there were calls from reporters, Montgomery Improvement Association staff, people wanting information, but the Kings never knew whether the caller would be a friend – or someone who would spit into the phone and threaten them with death.

Meeting hatred with love

Then, one day, the threats became real. King was speaking to a mass meeting when he was told that his house had been bombed. Numb with fear he rushed home; Coretta and the baby were safe. A bomb had been thrown onto the front porch. The explosion had shattered windows and split the porch in two, but no one had been hurt.

A crowd had gathered outside the house; it seemed to black people that an attack on their leader was an attack on each one of them. When the police tried to disperse them, they became angry. Dr. King was worried when he saw that many had weapons, guns, knives, broken bottles.

The police chief and the mayor arrived, full of apologies, but the people were not to be placated. They knew this bombing had been the inevitable result of the mayor's get-tough policy. The situation was becoming ugly, but at that moment Dr. King came out of the house.

"My wife and baby are all right. I want you all to go home and put away your weapons. We cannot

Above: The demonstrations were met with anger and hatred. When King led his people by kneeling in prayer, hundreds of bystanders shrieked, "Hate! Hate! Hate!"

Left: Whites lined the roadsides during marches, heckling the columns of marchers. Some posters declared "Segregation forever," "Communist Jews behind race mix," and "Go home to Africa."

Coretta King with her youngest daughter, Bunny. When he was courting Coretta, Martin told her, "The four things I look for in a wife are character, intelligence, personality and beauty. And you have them all."

Right: Coretta with Bunny, Marty and Yoki.

Coretta with Martin on one of the many marches he led. Coretta stood by Martin through these dangerous years. Despite death threats, she kept the home serene and happy. She was kept busy backing-up Martin's pastoral care of his Dexter Avenue parish. At other times, she would be by his side during the most frightening hours of his demonstrations.

Coretta King's verdict on her husband was simple, "He was good – such a very good man." Despite all his fame, she says, "he was a truly humble man and never felt adequate to his positions. That is why he worried so much, worked so hard, studied constantly, long after he became a world figure."

solve this problem through retaliatory violence. We must meet hatred with love."

"Remember," he said, "if I am stopped, this movement will not stop, because God is with this movement."

The explosive moment had passed. King had regained control; the people began to drift away. A white policeman who had been there that night said later that he owed his life "to that nigger preacher and so do all the other white people who were there."

The walking goes on

The boycott went on. There seemed no end in sight. Yet all that hard winter, the black people went on walking. The city was determined to defeat them and searched out an old, state anti-boycott law. Under it, eighty-nine people, including King, were charged. King was the first to be tried and convicted by an all-white jury, but his lawyers filed an appeal and the trial of the others was put off until a higher court could hear his case.

Meanwhile, the Improvement Association was

"There was never a moment when we were not united in our love and dedication, never a moment that I wanted to be anything but the wife of Martin Luther King."

Coretta Scott-King,
from "My Life With
Martin Luther King."

continuing to fight to prove that bus segregation was against the Constitution of the United States, a slow legal process but their only hope.

The months passed, and still the black people walked, on and on through the sweltering heat of the southern summer.

The city made a new determined effort to stop the car pool as a "public nuisance." How could the boycott endure another winter if the car pool was broken? Even Martin Luther King himself was beginning to feel drained of hope.

The Supreme Court ruling

Dejected, he was in court listening to the representatives of the City attacking the car-pool, when a reporter appeared at his elbow.

"This is what you've been waiting for!" he said. It was a message off the wire service.

"The United States Supreme Court today affirmed a US District Court decision declaring Alabama's state and civil laws requiring segregation on the buses unconstitutional."

The quiet, determined fight by the Montgomery Improvement Association had been victorious. There was nothing the racist whites of Montgomery could do. It no longer mattered that the court ruled that the car pool was to be suspended. The blacks didn't need it any more.

There was no magical change. The black people had to wait until the official court order reached the town. Martin Luther King knew his opponents; he knew they would not submit quietly.

The Ku Klux Klan paraded the streets, but the black people watched them instead of hiding away. They had learned new courage. They needed it. When the time came for them to go back to using the buses, they had to face vicious attacks by white militants. Mobs dragged black passengers off the buses, a young girl was badly beaten, and a pregnant woman was shot and wounded in both legs.

Not only gunfire threatened them, but bombs. The Baptist Church that had so often been the rallying point for the boycotters was burned. On

the same night three other black Montgomery churches were bombed as well as the houses of two ministers who had supported the protests.

Later, a bundle of smoking dynamite was found on the porch of King's house. The "superior" white race was trying to prove its superiority by using the methods of thugs and gangsters.

Martin Luther King was the first black passenger to board a bus. His companion was Rosa Parks, the courageous lady who had begun it all – along with leaders, black and white, who had fought so long and hard for this day.

As King boarded the bus, the white driver said, "I believe you are Reverend King, aren't you?" "Yes I am," King replied. "We're glad to have you with us this morning."

They smiled at each other.

The mixed group of white and black passengers settled themselves – and Montgomery's first integrated bus pulled away from the stop.

"We are on the move now," said King in one speech, "and no wave of racism can stop us. And the burning of our churches will not divert us.... We are on the move now. Like an idea whose time has come, not even the marching of mighty armies can stop us. We're moving to the land of freedom." "Freedom" was the watchword, the songs were of "freedom," the signs were for "freedom."

Above: Martin Luther King, Jr., with his son, Dexter Scott.

Right: With his oldest son, Martin Luther King, III, after church.

"My husband often told the children that if a man had nothing that was worth dying for, then he was not fit to live. He said also that it's not how long you live, but how well you live."
Coretta Scott-King, from "My Life with Martin Luther King."

Wider and wider

The success in Montgomery was only a beginning. It gave courage to thousands of other black people all across the South, and protests and boycotts sprang up everywhere.

But to be successful they needed to work together. In January 1957, the Southern Christian Leadership Conference (SCLC) was founded to advise and help them and Martin Luther King was made president.

But fame brought problems. King was in tremendous demand as a speaker, and he felt it was his duty to do everything in his power to help spread the message of the civil rights campaign. At times,

Above: Playing baseball with Martin III.

Left: Moments of happiness in the garden, throwing his youngest daughter, Bunny, high in the air.
King sometimes had four or five meetings or speaking engagements a day. But in his snatched moments at home, he laughed and played with his children.

his schedule seemed simply impossible. In 1957 and 1958 he journeyed thousands of miles, giving 208 speeches all over the country. Somehow he had to fit in his work as a minister and also as president of SCLC. On top of that, he had promised a New York publisher to write a book on the Montgomery boycott. He longed sometimes to be at home with his wife and children. They had two now, and it was hard to miss so much of their growing up. Somehow, despite all the travel and stress, the family remained close and loving.

He did not dare slow down, despite his utter exhaustion between engagements. With the success of Montgomery still fresh in everyone's minds, he *had* to push home his message. It was a bewildering life: one week he might be imprisoned in a jail on a civil rights issue and the next he would be a distinguished celebrity in New York, signing copies of his book *Stride Toward Freedom.*

A sneeze from death

It was when he was autographing the book, that a middle-aged black woman came up to him and asked, "Are you Martin Luther King?"

"Yes, I am."

An ordinary, polite exchange of words, yet this time it was different. The woman let out a cry and plunged a razor-sharp letter opener into his chest. She was a homeless vagrant who had spent years in and out of mental hospitals.

Dr. King was rushed to the hospital, and after a long, long wait, the knife was surgically removed. Mercifully, he had obeyed the nurses and kept absolutely still, despite the pain and shock, for the tip of the knife was a fraction of an inch from a major artery. The surgeon later said that one sneeze would have killed him.

The incident was reported in the newspapers and King was particularly pleased to read a letter written to him by a fifteen-year-old.

"Dear Dr. King,

I am a ninth grade student at the White Plains High School. While it shouldn't matter, I would like to mention that I am a white girl. I read in the paper of your misfortune and your suffering, and I read that if you had sneezed you would have died.

I'm simply writing to say that I'm so happy you didn't sneeze."

Such signs of affection and friendship made it possible to go on – that, and the love and understanding of Coretta and the family that meant so much to him.

Later that year King submitted his resignation to the Dexter Avenue Baptist Church. He and Coretta moved the family to Atlanta, where Dr. King became co-pastor, with his father, of the Ebenezer Baptist Church.

"I think the greatest victory of this period was ... something internal. The real victory was what this period did to the psyche of the black man. The greatness of this period was that we armed ourselves with dignity and self-respect. The greatness of this period was that we straightened our backs up. And a man can't ride your back unless it's bent."

Martin Luther King, Jr.

The student movement

Buses had been only one problem. In 1960, a black college student was refused service at a bus-terminal lunch counter and joined with two other students in staging a protest. They were determined to follow the example of non-violence that had been so successful in Montgomery.

Day after day, they went back to sit at the counter. More and more students joined them. They were insulted. They were never served. They sat on.

When newspapers began to report the story, other sit-ins started throughout the South. The students set up the Student Non-Violent Coordinating Committee (SNCC) to give each other support. Martin Luther King gave them every encouragement, joining them in some of their sit-ins. During a sit-in in Atlanta, he was arrested with seventy-five other demonstrators. The students were released after a few days. The police kept King in jail.

Three days later, King's case came to trial. Coretta, pregnant with their third child, attended the hearing with Daddy King. It was a dreadful shock to the family to hear the judge pronounce: "I find the defendant guilty and sentence him to four months hard labor at the state penitentiary."

It was a vindictive and outrageously heavy sentence for such a "crime" – a peaceful demonstration that had injured no one. Chained and handcuffed, King was driven to the state penitentiary, where he was shut alone into a small, filthy cell, alive with cockroaches.

Help from JFK

The next morning, Coretta received a telephone call. It was Senator John F. Kennedy, the Democratic candidate in the current presidential election. He said he had been shocked to hear of her husband's sentence and offered his help. Coretta accepted the offer gladly and a few days later was overjoyed to hear that the judge had reversed his decision. Soon, Martin was home again, and a crowd of happy supporters was waiting outside to welcome him.

"The nonviolent approach does not immediately change the heart of the oppressor. It first does something to the hearts and souls of those committed to it. It gives them new self-respect; it calls up resources of strength and courage that they did not know they had. Finally it reaches the opponent and so stirs his conscience that reconciliation becomes a reality."
    Martin Luther King, Jr.

The remains of the first Freedom Riders' bus. When the bus reached Anniston, Alabama, an angry white mob, armed with iron bars, smashed the bus, set it on fire and beat up the passengers. Nine white men were subsequently arrested, but went unpunished.

Kennedy's help did more than free Martin Luther King. His opponent in the race for the Presidency, Richard Nixon, had been silent on the issue of civil rights. In consequence, many black people gave Kennedy their vote. It may be that his support of Martin Luther King won JFK the Presidency.

The Freedom Riders

During the summer of 1961, groups of black and white students from the North set out to travel south by bus, staging sit-ins at bus terminals and restaurants along the way. They called themselves "Freedom Riders."

Southern racists were even more angry than they had been when confronted by local students. They felt these Freedom Riders had no right to interfere in southern issues. Even some older people in the established civil rights movement were very worried by the action. The students seemed to be asking for trouble.

The first Freedom Ride began well, but when the students reached Alabama, they were confronted by a group of Klansmen, armed with lead pipes and baseball bats. The unarmed students were severely beaten, and another group narrowly escaped death when the bus was set on fire.

The violence of this attack on peaceful demonstrators disturbed Martin Luther King deeply. He decided the students needed his help.

One evening he was speaking in a church in Montgomery asking for support for the Freedom Riders, when he was told that a mob of white extremists had gathered outside. Just as he received the message, there was a glare of flame at the windows. The roar of fire filled the air. The mob had set the cars outside ablaze. Fear swept through the congregation; no one knew what might happen next. Suddenly, a rain of stones shattered the windows, followed by gas bombs. Everyone began to cough and gasp for breath. It seemed as if the peaceful street had been plunged into war. For a while it looked as though Dr. King and the congregation would be trapped inside the church and burned alive.

But the law could still prevail, even in Montgomery. A group of National Guard soldiers arrived just in time to put down the riot and help the people inside the church to safety. Once again, Dr. King had escaped death. But for how long?

The end of Jim Crow

The violence that met the Freedom Riders that summer rose to new levels, but reporters and cameramen were there, running great risks to get their stories. At last, the world saw the terrible things that ordinary men and women were suffering in the cause of equality. The courage of the Freedom Riders had an effect, at last, on public opinion.

Because of their bravery, the despicable racist Jim Crow laws were dealt a decisive blow. The US government ruled that segregation at bus stations must come to an end. Martin Luther King recognized the debt he owed those reporters.

"Without the presence of the press there might have been untold massacre in the South. The world seldom believes the horror stories of history until they are documented via the mass media."

When the Freedom Riders reached Montgomery, James Zwerg, a student from Wisconsin, was mercilessly beaten up. He made no attempt to fight back. No white ambulances would go to the assistance of the Freedom Riders, so Zwerg had to wait patiently for a black ambulance.

41

Confrontation Birmingham

"Segregation now, segregation tomorrow, segregation forever!" was the slogan that helped elect George Wallace governor of Alabama in November 1962. Victories won by black people in other parts of the country had made the racist whites of Alabama more determined than ever to keep things going in the age-old ways of their forefathers. But Martin Luther King and the Southern Christian Leadership Conference were equally determined, although they knew that in taking on Birmingham, Alabama, they were taking on southern racism at its very worst.

The protest sit-ins and boycotts began in April of 1963. Their aim was to force the city to employ blacks in better jobs and to stop segregation.

"Bull" Connor, the white Commissioner of Public Safety of Birmingham, was a local celebrity. Some white people thought his country ways and rough opinions made him a distinctive local character, but his coarse jokes were matched by his bigotry. He had many admirers – people who agreed with his determination to prevent any form of integration. He declared that "blood would run in the streets" of the city before it would see desegregation. To him, every black person was and always would be a "nigger."

Opposite: King in jail in Birmingham, Alabama. Putting his Gandhian ideas into practice, King and his campaigners marched in wave after wave upon Birmingham City Hall, ignoring threats of arrest. Singing "We Shall Overcome," "Ain't Gonna Let Nobody Turn Me Round," and "Woke Up This Morning With My Mind Stayed on Freedom," marcher after marcher was arrested. Eventually, with more than nine hundred people in jail, the city authorities realized that it would be impossible to jail everyone.

Letter from Birmingham Jail

During the first really big march, on April 12, Dr. King was arrested and taken to Birmingham Jail. He was used to jail by now and knew, even behind bars, that the love and support of his people were with him. It was hard for Coretta, but this was the man she had married, and she was proud of him.

While he was in jail, a group of white churchmen wrote to the local paper, criticizing what was going on. They said Dr. King was an outsider and was just stirring up trouble. They urged black people to give up demonstrating.

Dr. King was deeply hurt. How could he reply when he was forbidden to have writing paper. He collected together any scraps of paper he could find

– bags, toilet paper, the margins of newspapers – and he wrote down all he believed. This was to become known as "Letter from a Birmingham Jail," one of the most important documents of the civil rights movement.

He had been called an outside agitator. He wrote: "I am in Birmingham because injustice is here, and injustice is a universal thing – nothing to do with 'insiders' or 'outsiders.'"

He explained that demonstrations were vital, that non-violent action on a big scale *forced* people to admit something was wrong, and to deal with it.

Left to themselves, people would never change. He denied that the demonstrations were untimely. Demands for justice were always untimely to the oppressor. Every black person was constantly being told to wait, and he believed that "wait" was simply another word for "never."

He quoted a famous lawyer, "Justice too long delayed is justice too long denied."

Bull Connor attacks

Soon, Dr. King was released and set out to appeal to students to give their support to the cause. To his astonishment, not only students came forward, but little children too. Remembering his own children, he thought very seriously about what he should do. But after all, it was the future of these children that was at stake. They had a right to join the demonstrations.

As a result, so many children were arrested for marching in the demonstration of May 2, 1963, that school buses had to be used to take them to jail. Young people of 16 and 17 paraded alongside little children of six.

The next day, young people gathered at the Sixteenth Street Baptist Church to march again. One thousand children set off for downtown Birmingham chanting, "We want freedom." They were met by all the law-enforcement might Bull Connor could summon.

When Connor ordered them to turn back, they ignored him. Again he ordered them to stop – but

they continued their march. Suddenly, Connor gave his men the order to attack. Firemen trained their powerful hoses on the marchers; the great jets of water hit the protesters with the impact of a giant fist. Children were toppled over like pieces of paper, their clothes ripped by the force of the water. Battered and bloodied, they were pushed backward. Inevitably, some protesters, driven to fury by this heartless attack, broke away from the confusion and began to hurl anything they could at the police. All reason seemed to desert Connor's men. The police let loose their dogs, which plunged into the crowd, snarling and snapping at the children as they tried to get away. Bull Connor laughed aloud. "Look at those niggers run."

But all the time the television cameras were turning. The grinning police, the snarling dogs, the terrified marchers flung to the ground by the force of the water jets – and it was all being recorded.

The next day people all across the country saw those scenes. They were horrified.

A victory for non-violence

As Martin Luther King had said "We will match your capacity to inflict suffering by our capacity to endure suffering."

Those scenes in Birmingham shocked the world. And still the marchers refused to give in. Every day the demonstrators returned to the streets, knowing full well what they faced. They marched up to the waiting police, the dogs, the high pressure hoses, singing their songs of freedom.

And then – on May 5, 1963 – something strange and wonderful happened.

Black clergymen were leading a public march to Birmingham Jail, singing hymns as they went, when the demonstrators came at last to the police lines that barred their path. Quietly they all stopped and knelt to pray for a few moments. Then they moved forward.

Connor was there.

"Turn on the hoses," he yelled. "Damn you, turn on the hoses."

But the police and firemen made no move. They looked at the quiet faces before them, the harmless gentle people who had done nothing to merit abuse.

The police moved back and let the company of protesters through.

Connor stood stunned and powerless. His troops had abandoned him.

Martin Luther King's faith in the fundamental goodness to be found in most men had been justified. Non-violence had triumphed, though at a high cost in suffering. Over 3,000 demonstrators had been arrested during the protests.

Bull Connor and Abe Lincoln

The sheer size and determination of the demonstrations had worn the city down, even though the officials would still not admit defeat. White business people agreed to allow black people equal opportunities with white, and an inter-racial committee was set up to work out community problems.

The rule of prejudice and bigotry was broken. The Birmingham Campaign cost Bull Connor his job; he was voted out of the office at the next election. More important, it forced the federal government to take action to protect civil rights.

President Kennedy proposed a new Civil Rights Bill to the United States Congress, remarking later that "Bull Connor has done as much for civil rights as Abraham Lincoln!"

Connor's rabid bigotry had forced ordinary people who had never before thought much about black people's rights into making a stand for justice.

The 1963 march on Washington

After the hard-won Birmingham campaign, a march on Washington was organized. It took place on August 28, 1963 and commemorated the one-hundredth anniversary of the abolition of slavery in the States.

Martin Luther King hoped that 100,000 people would gather in the heart of Washington. But the television reports that morning had spoken of a crowd of only 25,000. If too few people came, no one would believe in the importance of the campaign for civil rights.

A lot of the young marchers marked their foreheads with an "equality sign" to show their total commitment.

When he and Coretta were driven to where the marchers were gathering, their hearts stopped for a moment. They could see the crowd before them. The whole scene was alive with people, black and white, moving together. Not 25,000 but 250,000 people – and not a single sign of violence.

Martin Luther King left the car and joined the crowd as it moved over the grass to the Lincoln Memorial, singing "We Shall Overcome," carrying posters that spoke of their cause.

"We seek the freedom in 1963 promised in 1863."

"A century-old debt to pay."

Many important men spoke to the crowds that day as they stood before the great white pillars of the Lincoln Memorial. It looked as if the huge, seated figure of Abraham Lincoln, that advocator of freedom, listened to them.

Martin Luther King was 34, still a young man, but to that vast assembly he was the figure that stood for all they believed.

He had planned his speech carefully. So much depended on his finding the right words, the words to meet the moment, the words to change people's minds, the words to change people's hearts.

He began by speaking of the promise of equality as a bad debt that the government had yet to settle, a promise of payment that had led to nothing.

The crowd hung on his words. He could feel their unity, their support. As he went on they applauded and called out in agreement. He knew that he was speaking with their voice – speaking for them as well as to them.

"I have a dream"

Lifted on the wave of their response, he put aside the notes for his speech and spoke from his heart. And from his heart came the greatest speech of the civil rights movement, the speech that has become a part of history.

"I say to you today, my friends, that in spite of the difficulties and frustrations of the moment I still have a dream. I have a dream that one day this nation will rise up and live out the true meaning

of its creed: 'We hold these truths to be self-evident: that all men are created equal.'

"I have a dream that one day on the red hills of Georgia the sons of former slaves and the sons of former slave-owners will be able to sit down together at the table of brotherhood.

"I have a dream that one day even the state of Mississippi will be transformed into an oasis of freedom and justice.

Martin Luther King, speaking in Washington, at the Memorial to Abraham Lincoln, who had abolished slavery just one hundred years previously. Giving the finest speech of his life, King ended, "When we let freedom ring, when we let it ring from every village and every hamlet, from every state and every city, we will be able to speed up that day when all of God's children, black men and white men, Jews and Gentiles, Protestants and Catholics, will be able to join hands and sing in the words of the old Negro spiritual, 'Free at last! Free at last! Thank God almighty, we are free at last!'"

"I have a dream that my four little children will one day live in a nation where they will not be judged by the color of their skin, but by the content of their character."

The vast crowd understood. This was no ordinary speech – this was a message that reached out to all people, of every belief and background.

"This will be the day when all of God's children will be able to sing with new meaning 'My country 'tis of thee let freedom ring.'

"And if America is to be a great nation, this must become true. So let freedom ring from the prodigious hilltops of New Hampshire. Let freedom ring from the mighty mountains of New York. But not only that. Let freedom ring from every hill and molehill of Mississippi....

"When we let freedom ring from every town and every hamlet, from every state and every city, we will be able to speed up that day when all God's children, black men and white men, Jews and Gentiles, Protestants and Catholics, will be able to join hands and sing in the words of that old Negro spiritual, 'Free at last! Free at last! Thank God almighty, we are free at last.'"

The crowd roared in response as he finished. He had given voice to the longing of all those involved in the civil rights movement for the unity of black and white Americans, the unification of the nation.

On that day, many newspapers reported that King had become the unofficial "President of Black America." He was now the acknowledged leader of the civil rights movement, a man trusted and loved by his followers and respected by people everywhere. It had been a great day in his life and the history of the United States.

A hope too soon

When Dr. King spoke in Washington of his dream of peace and unity, it seemed that perhaps the victory of Birmingham could be extended, by the same non-violent means, to transform the whole country.

But that hope came too soon. Only a few weeks

later, the 16th Street Baptist Church in Birmingham was bombed.

Inside the church, children were attending Sunday School. Suddenly a car roared down the street outside, and a bomb was flung against the building. A great hole was torn in the wall, and the windows exploded into thousands of flying fragments of glass. Four young girls between eleven and thirteen years old – members of the church choir – were killed. Many, many others were injured. They poured out into the street, sobbing with terror, the debris of the blast spattered with blood.

It was only a month later – on November 22, 1963 – that the nation and the world were stunned by the assassination of President John F. Kennedy – shot dead as he and his wife were being driven through the streets of Dallas, Texas.

Martin Luther King was among the millions who mourned him as they watched the scenes of his assassination and funeral on television.

He was filled with foreboding. US society had become so violent. At every turn, one could read of murder, assassination, guns. Dr. King knew that only too often one assassination triggered another. Every violent death made the possibility of other deaths more likely.

Now he knew. "That is what is going to happen to me," he said.

"Support Your Local Police"

Integrated buses and lunch counters, equality at work – they were'all victories, but still there was so much to do.

Kennedy was dead and the campaign to find a new president was under way. Kennedy's former vice-president, Lyndon Johnson, was running against Barry Goldwater, a man who liked things to stay just as they were. It was vital for civil rights that black Americans be able to vote so that they could choose a President who would help their cause. The students' civil rights movement was determined that they should have that chance.

"Few can explain the extraordinary King mystique. Yet he has an indescribable capacity for empathy that is the touchstone of leadership. By deed and by preachment, he has stirred in his people a Christian forbearance that nourishes hope and smothers injustice."

"Time Magazine," January 3, 1964, on naming King the Man of the Year for 1963.

In Mississippi they made great steps to achieving their goal, but at terrible cost. Three young workers, two white and one black, had been trying to ensure the registration of black voters. In June of 1964, they were arrested. After that, nothing whatsoever was heard of them until August, when their bodies were found. They had been hanged.

Eventually two men were brought to trial on a charge of conspiracy in the lynch murders – Sheriff Lawrence Rainey of Neshoba County and his deputy, Cecil Price. A photographer for *Life* magazine took photographs of them in court. Fat, smiling, they lolled among their grinning cronies. To all of them the proceedings were a huge joke; they were quite certain that they would go free. Rainey was acquitted, Price given only a six year sentence. But the photograph was made into a poster that spoke for civil rights and justice. Across it was the sarcastic message "Support Your Local Police."

Getting out the vote

In October 1964, Dr. King received the Nobel Peace Prize, one of the world's highest awards. But he hardly stopped to draw breath. He felt it was now vital to concentrate on one key spot. He and his workers chose Selma, Alabama.

By pooling all their resources, they were determined to get the black people of Selma the vote that was rightfully theirs.

Dr. King launched the campaign in January 1965. "We are going to start a march on the ballot boxes in thousands," he said. "We must be willing to go to jail by thousands. We are not asking, we are demanding the ballot."

On paper, blacks had the vote, but they had to register. But when they tried, the application office closed or a fault was found in their forms. By the beginning of February, 280 people had been arrested trying to register to vote. Only 57 had succeeded in getting as far as completing forms. *None had been registered.*

They had been forbidden by the authorities to march, so instead they walked to the county court-

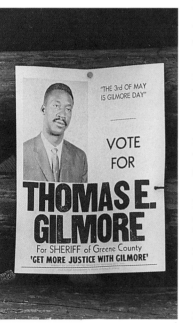

Voting for the first time in Greene County, Alabama.

house in disciplined groups, led by Dr. King, so that the police could have no excuse to stop them. Nevertheless, they were arrested.

Dr. King wrote from jail.

"There are more Negroes in jail with me than there are on the voting rolls."

The protests went on. At one peaceful demonstration, a young man named Jimmie Lee Jackson was shot dead by state troops. Members of the press were there. A wave of indignation swept the country. But the brutality went on, the troops continuing to attack the protesters and the cameramen with clubs, whips and tear gas.

A long march from Selma to Montgomery was planned, but the state police met them on their way. They rode their horses straight into the crowd, beating, whipping and clubbing the protesters as they fell beneath the horses' hooves.

Only a few days later, a white minister from Boston was attacked and killed by the KKK in Selma. Public demands for federal government support grew. President Johnson responded and, condemning the violence, began to prepare a new Voting Rights Bill.

On July 2, 1964, President Johnson signed the Civil Rights Act and went on television to declare that, "those who are equal before God shall now be equal in the polling booths, in the classrooms, in the factories, and in hotels, restaurants, movie theaters, and other places that provide services to the public."

At last the "WHITES ONLY" signs would be torn down, and black people would be able to stand for mayor, sheriff and all other public offices in the local communities.

Above: The state troopers brandishing night sticks barred the road to the unarmed marchers. Seventeen people were seriously injured.

Opposite: "I do not know what lies ahead of us," King told the marchers the next day. "There may be beatings, jailings, and tear gas. But I would rather die on the highways of Alabama than make a butchery of my conscience."
Fifteen hundred marchers again faced the police. Under King's leadership, they prayed and then turned back. Not one was hurt.

On the move

On March 21, the demonstrators were at last given permission to march from Selma to Montgomery, with Dr. King leading them. He had returned to the city where he'd seen the beginning of the civil rights movement 10 years before.

"Today I want to say to the people of America and the nations of the world that we are not about to turn around. We are on the move now and no wave of racism can stop us. We're moving to the land of freedom."

Because of Selma, the Voting Rights Bill of 1965 came into force, which gave the federal government the power to see that voting was fair and free of discrimination. It abolished all the technical tricks that had been used to prevent black people from having the vote.

Up North

Life for black people away from the southern states was not a bed of roses. In the cities of the North, there were black ghetto areas, places of dilapidated housing, poverty, unemployment, bad schooling. Often this led to violence, drug abuse, drunkenness, gang warfare, crime.

Non-violence seemed too soft a method to use in such conditions, but Dr. King was sure it could work. Many other black leaders disagreed. The militant Black Power Movement was gaining followers. They were tired of oppression and were determined to break it by a show of strength. Speeches and posters told the black people to strike out against the whites, to seize what was rightly theirs. Rioting broke out, fires, looting, mayhem. The riots spread from Chicago, erupting in Boston, Los

By no means did all black people share the views of Martin Luther King. Impatient with the progress being made, a close friend of King's, Stokely Carmichael, began a militant anti-white campaign. He was the first person to use the Black Power slogan.

Angeles, Philadelphia, city after city.

Dr. King condemned such violence, but he knew why it existed. He explained to the people in power what it was like to live in ghettos, in ugliness and poverty and frustration. Ghettos could never be peaceful as long as ghettos were allowed to exist.

The Promised Land

The riots were not the States' only problem. In April 1968, Dr. King went to Memphis to give his support to workers fighting for equal pay.

The airport officials were worried. There had been so much violence that they feared a bomb might be planted on the plane and delayed the flight while they searched it. All was well, but Dr. King was late for his meeting. To cheers he stepped up on to the platform.

He told his audience why he was late and that he had had many threats on his life. He spoke of the ever-present danger of assassination.

"Like anybody," he said, "I would like to live a long life. But I am not concerned about that now. I just want to do God's will. And He's allowed me to go up to the mountain. And I've looked over and I've seen the promised land. I may not get there with you. But I want you to know tonight that we as a people will get to the promised land. And I'm happy tonight. I'm not worried about anything. I'm not fearing any man. Mine eyes have seen the glory of the coming of the Lord."

His speech was prophetic. It was as if he had prepared himself to die and put all fear behind him.

Martin Luther King spent most of the following day in his hotel room, working out the details of the protest action. Once more he emphasized to his friends that they must at all costs avoid violence. Non-violence must, as always, be the rule, *whatever the provocation.*

That evening they went out onto the hotel balcony to stretch their legs. Suddenly there was a sharp explosion. Dr. King reeled and then pitched to the ground. A shot had been fired from the roof of a nearby building.

His friends rushed to him, but the bullet had exploded in his neck. He was very badly hurt.

He was rushed to the hospital but an hour later he was dead.

This time the bayonets are <u>*protecting*</u> *the demonstrators as they march through Memphis, Tennessee, to demand equality in wages for black and white sanitation workers.*

The death of non-violence?

Martin Luther King's death came as a terrible blow.

The nation and workers for peace across the world mourned him. For many black Americans he had been the only hope in their world of poverty and humiliation. And now he was gone.

Stokeley Carmichael, the young black militant, declared, "When white America killed Dr. King last night, she declared war on us. He was the one man in our race who was trying to teach our people to have love, compassion and mercy for white people."

That last day of his life, Martin Luther King had spoken of his way of peace, Gandhi's way of peace – non-violence. But the violence of his end triggered a great wave of black riots across the country.

Thirty-nine people died in the looting and gunfire

REV. MARTIN LUTHER KING JR.
1929 ——— 1968
"FREE AT LAST, FREE AT LAST,
THANK GOD ALMIGHTY I'M FREE AT LAST."

Oppressed people all over the world were deeply shocked and saddened by Martin Luther King's murder. About 120 million Americans watched the funeral of Martin Luther King. On his tombstone, cut in the marble, were the words of the old slave spiritual, "Free at last."

Opposite: Coretta King at her husband's funeral.

"The day that Negro people and others in bondage are truly free, on the day when want is abolished, on the day wars are no more, on that day I know my husband will rest in a long-deserved peace."

Coretta Scott-King, from "My Life with Martin Luther King."

---

of those riots, the very thing that Martin Luther King, Jr. had lived and died to prevent.

President Johnson said: "No one could doubt what Martin Luther King would want. That his death should be the cause for more violence would deny everything that he worked for."

Free at last

Black America mourned along with his wife and children, who had had a loving husband and father snatched away from them.

The funeral was held at the Baptist Church in Atlanta where he had preached his very first sermon. His had not been a long life; he was only 39. But his life had changed the lives of thousands.

Over 100,000 people gathered to pay tribute to him. Like a great river, they flowed behind the wagon, drawn by two mules, that carried his coffin to the grave.

Just as the mule wagon reminded his people of their beginnings, so too did the inscription on his gravestone. It was a quotation from an old spiritual, the song from the heart of the slaves that he had quoted in his great speech in Washington.

"Free at last, free at last. Thank God Almighty, I'm free at last."

Background information about black people in the United States

Slavery is almost as old as civilization itself. The great early civilizations were all based on the backs of innumerable slaves, and slaves were common throughout feudal Europe as late as AD 1200. In Central and South America, the Spanish conquerors, the conquistadors enslaved millions of native Americans to work their lands and serve in their homes, following the example of the Inca and Aztecs.

However, it was with the "discovery" of the Americas by Christopher Columbus in 1492, that slavery really became big business. Black peoples were brought in from the west coast of Africa. They were used to the heat, they were hard workers and they were easy to control, so that they would enable the settlers to become wealthy by running vast plantations. The first recorded cargo of African slaves arrived in 1518. Between then and 1865 when slavery was abolished officially, it is estimated that over fifteen million men, women and children were shipped across the Atlantic.

Very few of these people were kidnapped by the European sailors – the vast majority were enslaved by their own rulers or by conquerors from neighbouring tribes. This trade was very profitable for those kings who lived on the coasts. They were paid in "trade goods": mostly fabrics, knives, swords, guns and ammunition, iron bars, brass bedsteads, fancy hats, glass beads and well-watered liquor.

Slavers argued about the best way to transport their human cargo; most favoured the "tight-packed" method which allowed each adult male a space six feet long by sixteen inches wide; an adult woman five feet ten inches by sixteen inches; a boy five feet by fourteen inches, and a girl four feet six inches by one foot. The more humane captains allowed them out on deck while the holds were cleaned, but many left them in that tiny space for the entire voyage which could last up to three months. The losses on the voyages were frightful: 100 to 130 dead out of 150 were not uncommon. One ship is recorded as landing 85 out of a cargo of 390!

After 1713, Great Britain became the premier slaving nation, transporting about seventy thousand people per year to the West Indies and North America. It can reasonably be said that Britain's Industrial Revolution was built on the profits of slavery, which were enormous.

Great Britain abolished slavery within the British Isles in 1772, when Lord Chief Justice Mansfield handed down his historic decision that "as soon as any slave sets foot on English ground, he becomes free."

The Founding Fathers of the United States included slaves among those goods which they would not import in 1774, and the trade was halted until 1783. They would have abolished slavery completely but two states – South Carolina and Georgia – held out against this threat to their economies. All northern states abolished slavery early on – the last was New Jersey in 1804. However the South insisted that the principle of slavery should be permitted in the new states that were being added to the Union after 1845.

From about 1830 onwards, there was a steady, if not very effective, rumbling from the North demanding total abolition of slavery. Then, in 1861, eleven southern states formed the Confederacy and broke away from the United States over abolition. The American Civil War, between the North and South, followed. After four years of fighting and over half a million deaths, the North won. The Emancipation Proclamation was passed and now, at last, the slaves were free.

But that was in theory only. For over a hundred years since the end of the war, the southern states had resisted national efforts to give black people an equal chance. The southern whites blamed the black people for the war, the defeat and the resulting poverty. Their leaders had tried to preserve their old way of life, their "heritage." And the black people, owning no land and having no education, had found progress almost impossible.

Sadly President Lincoln's assassination in April 1865 meant that the one chance to reconstruct the South in a new mould was lost. The old southern leaders were not excluded from office and so they were able to pass the "Black Codes" which denied black people all but the most basic civil rights and liberties. It was in response to this oppression that the 14th Amendment to the US Constitution, establishing the rights of black people to be US citizens and to equal protection under the law, came into effect in 1866. This was followed in March 1870 by the 15th Amendment which gave voting rights to all US citizens regardless of "race, color or previous condition of servitude."

However, the North more or less left the South to deal with black people as they wished. The result was that, by 1895, practically all blacks had been denied the vote. The situation reached its worst point about 1900 after the Ku Klux Klan was re-established; between 1889 and 1919 nearly three thousand black men and women were lynched.

In the 1950s, when Martin Luther King took over the leadership of the black civil rights movement, most blacks were still poor and under-educated. Progress was blocked at every turn. For example, even though black people were legally allowed to vote, so many obstacles – from red-tape to lynchings – had been placed in their way in the southern states, that only five per cent had been able to register.

Under King's leadership a great deal of progress was made. But today, twenty years after King's death, there is still much de facto segregation particularly in the southern rural areas. The law says there is now equality but the prejudiced whites just walk around the law. The restaurants used to be open only to whites. So, when the law made this illegal the restaurants simply closed. In many small southern towns there are now no bars, hairdressers or restaurants. And the desegregated government schools have only black pupils. All the white children have been taken out and sent to private schools.

There is real progress in some fields. Before the Voting Rights Act (1965) there were fewer than 200 black elected officials across the US; by 1970 there were 1469; by 1980 there were 4912 and by 1986 there

were over 6,500. This is only 1.3 per cent of the US's 490,000 elective offices. There are 289 black mayors, twenty-eight of whom run cities of more than 50,000.

Black family poverty has declined from about fifty-five per cent in 1959 to about thirty-one per cent in 1987; however in 1986 thirty-seven per cent of those receiving Food Stamps (these can be exchanged for food in shops) were black, as were forty-five per cent of youths in the Job Corps. In 1985 the average black family income was only fifty-five per cent of that of the average white family, and nearly forty-five per cent of all black families are headed by a woman. In 1987, The State of Black America said of black unemployment in the northern states: "In cities such as Detroit, Buffalo, Chicago and Cleveland, the gap between the labor market position of blacks – especially black males – and whites probably exceeds the highest levels that ever existed in the most racist of the South's cities."

On the upbeat side have been the success stories – Bill Cosby who, in 1987, was the highest paid entertainer in the world, pulled eighty-three million viewers for his TV series and made nearly a hundred million dollars. Jesse Jackson is another success story – he was a serious contender for the Democratic nomination for US President in 1988. There are pop stars like Michael Jackson and Tina Turner who pack rock concerts across the world. There are managers like Clifford R. Warren, the ex-Chancellor of the State University of New York, who became head of America's largest pension fund and industrialists, like Herman E. Valentine, Chairman & President of Systems Management America Corporation.

Finally, there are the thousands of ordinary black American people who have made it into the middle class as doctors, lawyers, bankers, managers and the other professions. It is estimated that by AD 2000 every third American will be non-white – this includes Asians, Hispanics and Blacks – with perseverance, education, and a little more push, Martin Luther King's great dream may yet come true before another twenty years have passed.

Glossary

Abolitionist: The name given to those who campaigned between about 1830 and the *Civil War* in the US for the total abolition of slavery. Some of them were ex-slaves; others were whites who felt that the slave system was morally wrong.

Black power: A slogan coined in 1964. It encapsulates the Negro activists' demand for control of the *civil rights movement* and the use of all black resources, including force, for the betterment of the black community.

Boycott: A voluntary refusal to deal with a person, service or goods.

Civil rights movement: A 1950s/1960s non-violent campaign for legal enforcement of the equal status of black Americans, as guaranteed by the 14th and 15th Amendments to the US Constitution. It was superseded by more violent methods when the 1964 Civil Rights Act failed to achieve immediate improvements.

Civil War: War between the Union (northern) states and the *Confederate States,* in the USA, over the issue of the abolition of slavery. It started in 1861 and ended in 1865 with the total defeat of the South.

Confederate States: The collective name given to the eleven States that broke away in 1861 over the abolition of slavery. These were Alabama, Arkansas, North and South Carolina, Florida, Georgia, Louisiana, Mississippi, Tennessee, Texas and Virginia. They were defeated in 1865 and reunited with the USA.

Desegregation: The process of ending the separate, inferior facilities for a recognizable racial or social group. It was first used in the USA in legal actions to end separate provision of education in the southern states; the *Supreme Court* ruled segregation illegal in 1954.

Discrimination: When a person or group of people is singled out for positive or negative treatment. In this case, black people were discriminated against negatively on the grounds of their race.

Equality, racial: Often a legal enactment to provide a basis for anti-discrimination measure: e.g. the US 15th Amendment, 1870; the British Race Relations Act, 1976.

Freedom Riders: A group of white and black Americans who rode the interstate buses in the southern States to protest *racism* and test the federal *desegregation* laws.

Gandhi, Mahatma (1869-1948): The Indian Hindu leader who pioneered techniques of *non-violent protest* in South Africa and India. As leader of the struggle for Indian Independence, he was revered by millions.

Integration: The process whereby a minority group mixes with, and is accorded equal rights to, the majority society. This is also referred to as *desegregation,* particularly in the United States.

Jim Crow laws: Any law relating to black *segregation.* "Jim Crow" was a popular music-hall song in the 1850s and became a generic name for black people.

Ku Klux Klan: A secret organization founded in the 1860s in the *Confederate States* by southern whites to fight black emancipation and northern domination. It was responsible for thousands of lynchings and other violent acts against Negroes, Jews and minority groups. It is still active, though less influential than in the 1960s when many law-officers were members.

N.A.A.C.P.: National Association for the Advancement of Colored People, founded in 1909 by W.E.B. Du Bois.

Non-violent protest: The technique pioneered by *Mahatma Gandhi* in South Africa and India. It involved a total refusal to use violence against the oppressors plus a campaign of civil disobedience against rules and laws perceived as unjust.

Racism: Hostility and unfair treatment to a different race or culture based on the prejudiced belief that one race is naturally superior to another.

S.C.L.C.: Southern Christian Leadership Conference, set up in 1957 under the leadership of King, "to bring the Negro masses into the freedom struggle by expanding 'the Montgomery way' across the south."

Segregation: The establishment by law or custom of separate, inferior facilities for ethnic or social groups as in the *Jim Crow laws* of the southern states. It was extended in the 1950s and 1960s to include the denial of voting and employment rights of the black population in the southern states of America.

S.N.C.C.: Student Non-violent Coordinating Committee, set up in 1960 to combat *segregation.*

Supreme Court: The highest US law court. The ultimate function of its nine judges is to decide whether any federal or state law violates any portion of the US Constitution.

Important Dates

1929   Jan 15: Martin Luther King, Jr. is born in Atlanta, Georgia.

1948   Martin is ordained to the Baptist ministry.
Martin enters the Crozer Theological Seminary in Pennsylvania. He begins to study the teaching of Mahatma Gandhi.

1953   Martin marries Coretta Scott in Marion, Alabama.

1954   Martin accepts the post as minister at Dexter Avenue Baptist Church, Montgomery, Alabama.

1955   Martin receives a Ph.D. degree in Theology from Boston University.
Dec 1: Mrs. Rosa Parks refuses to give up her bus seat to a white man and is arrested.
Dec 5: The year-long Montgomery bus boycott begins.

1956   Feb 21: Dr. King is jailed with others in the bus boycott.
June 4: A district court rules that racial segregation on city buses is illegal.
Nov 13: The Supreme Court upholds the district court's decision.
Dec 21: Buses in Montgomery are integrated.

1957   The first Civil Rights Act since the end of the Civil War is passed.

1960   The first "sit-in" protest to desegregate eating facilities is held by students in Greensboro, North Carolina. Dr. King supports the protest and is jailed. Senator John F. Kennedy intervenes and Dr. King is released.
The Student Non-Violent Coordinating Committee (S.N.C.C.) is founded.

1961   The first group of "Freedom Riders" try to introduce racial integration on Greyhound interstate buses. On arrival in Alabama, they are beaten up, thrown in jail and the bus is burned.

1963   In Birmingham, Alabama, Bull Connor orders the police to use dogs and fire hoses on the marching protesters.
Aug 28: The first large protest march is held in Washington D.C. where Dr. King delivers his "I have a dream" speech.

1965   March 7: A group of marchers is beaten by State patrolmen on the way to Montgomery, Alabama.
March 21-25: Protesters march on Montgomery, protected by Federal troops.

1966   Twenty-three people are killed and 725 injured during riots in Newark, New Jersey.
Forty-three die, and 324 are injured in the Detroit riots, the worst of the century.

1968   April 3: Dr. King's speech "I've Been to the Mountain Top," is delivered in Memphis, Tennessee.
April 4: Dr. King is assassinated by a sniper on the balcony of his motel in Memphis, Tennessee.

1993   Aug: The thirtieth anniversary of Martin Luther King's "I have a dream" speech is commemorated with a march in Washington D.C.. The rally for "Jobs, Justice and Peace" is attended by 75,000 people, including Coretta Scott-King and Rosa Parks.

Index

Further Reading

Dewart, Janet (ed): *The State of Black America 1987* (National Urban League,
  New York, 1987)
King, Martin Luther: *Stride Toward Freedom* (Harper & Row, New York, 1958)
Long, Richard A: *Black Americana* (Admiral Books, England, 1985)
Montgomery, Maureen: *Civil Rights in the USA* ("People Then and Now":
  Macdonald Educational, London, 1986)
Owen, RJ: *Free at Last* (Religious & Moral Education Press, Oxford, 1980)
Schulke, Flip (ed): *Martin Luther King, Jr. – a Documentary ... Montgomery
  to Memphis* (WW Norton & Co, New York & London, 1976)
Schulke, Flip & McPhee, Penelope O.: *King Remembered* (WW Norton & Co,
  New York & London, 1986)

J